Mommy and Daddy Are Divorced

Mommy and Daddy Are Divorced

*by Patricia Perry &
Marietta Lynch*

THE DIAL PRESS/New York

Published by The Dial Press
1 Dag Hammarskjold Plaza
New York, N.Y. 10017

Library of Congress Cataloging
in Publication Data

Perry, Patricia.
Mommy and daddy are divorced.

Summary: Two young boys try to understand
and cope with the confusion and pain
of their parents' divorce.
[1. Divorce—Fiction]
I. Lynch, Marietta, joint author.
II. Title.
PZ7.P43585Mo   [E]   77-86268
ISBN 0-8037-5770-0
ISBN 0-8037-5771-9 lib. bdg.

To the special people who helped
to make this book possible—
Marie Cotter, Nicky, Russell,
Dot, and Bob

I felt so excited I didn't want to eat my cereal. It was
Wednesday. The day Joey and I had been waiting for.
My father had the morning off and he was coming over.
When my parents got divorced, he moved away to a new
house and now he doesn't live with us anymore.

When the doorbell rang, I knew it was my dad. While he was talking with my mother downstairs, I hurried to change out of my pajamas.

"Hurry up, Ned! Daddy and Joey are out in the yard," my mother called up to me.

When I came outside, my father was giving Joey a piggy-back ride. Joey was so happy to see him.

Then Lisa and Martha came over and together we looked for butterflies in the tall grass in the backyard.

My father told us to move softly and quietly through the grass.

"Be careful, Ned," he said to me. "If you move too fast, you'll scare the butterfly and it will fly away."

When I got very close, I cupped my hands and scooped it up. I held it for a moment and then watched it fly away over the rocks.

Then I showed my father how I could climb.
He said, "You're up so high, Ned."
I like it when my father watches me.

Sometimes I like to be alone with my father, so when we came indoors we sat down together and he helped me build my model airplane. He read the directions to me and we put the wings on.

Then he said, "Maybe some other day we can fly the plane, Ned, but now I have to go to the lab."

I ran outside. "I never want to see you again!" I shouted.
Daddy held me close. He said he understood how angry
I was, and he told me that he loved me even though he didn't
live with us anymore. "Don't worry," he said. "I'll be back
on Saturday to take you and Joey to see the place where I
work."

Then my father said good-bye to Joey. But Joey cried and said, "No, don't go!"

Daddy put him on his lap and told Joey that he had to go but that he would be thinking about him. And on Saturday he would take us to see all the test tubes and instruments in his laboratory. That made Joey feel a little better.

But after Joey said good-bye, he still wasn't very happy.
My mother read Joey's favorite story to help him feel better.
But I kept on thinking. I don't like it when my father
goes away.

"Why did you have to get divorced anyway?" I asked
my mother.

She said, "Remember Daddy and I told you how we were too unhappy together? We made each other angry and we hurt each other's feelings. Remember how we used to argue so much?

"We made each other sad. It's better for us to be divorced, not to live together anymore. There will be times when you'll be unhappy about it. But some things will be the same as always and we'll still have good times together."

It was hot on Thursday and we splashed and played in our
pool in the backyard.

Joey and I made the see-saw go up and down.

Joey was silly and sprayed me with the hose.

When we came inside, my mother was busy working with
her clay. She likes to make things out of clay. She makes
pots and dishes and vases. I watched her as she rolled out
her clay.

"When will Daddy be here?" I asked.

"Not until Saturday," she said.

I went outside and picked Tiger up.

"Tiger, I guess you'll have to wait till Saturday to see Dad."

On Friday afternoon while my mother was drinking her tea, Joey asked for a sip. Then he said, "Why don't you drink coffee like my daddy?"

"Different people like different things," she said. "I like tea. Your father likes coffee. You know, tomorrow morning your daddy will be here to see you."

"We know," he said.

When Saturday finally came, my father and Joey and I walked to his office. We held hands as we went down the street together.

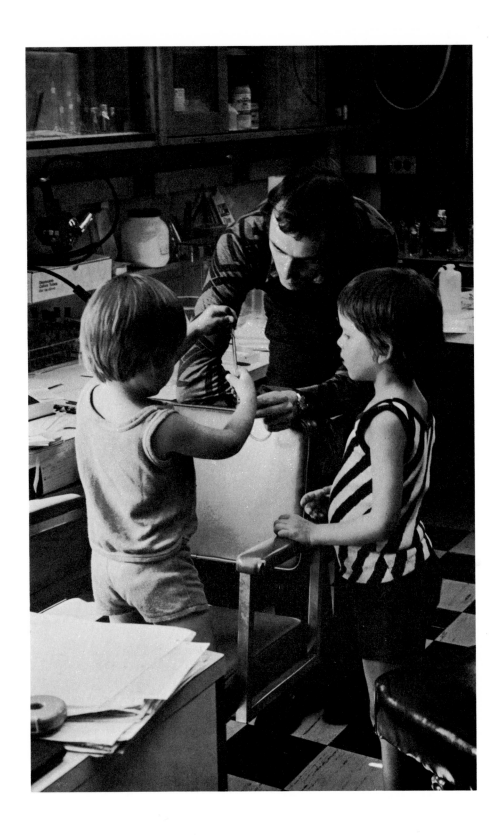

At the lab Joey tried out my father's chair and some of the instruments.

After we were finished, we walked home. We talked about all the special things we had seen. I was tired and cold and wanted to get home and put on my sweatshirt. It felt good to hold my father's hand.

We said good-bye on the front steps.

It didn't feel good to see Daddy go, but we knew that we would see him again soon. And we watched as he walked down the street to the bus stop.

JE
Per

Perry, Patricia

Mommy and Daddy are Divorced